Mêlée Live

No. 1

VOLUME 1

POCKET EDITION

Mêlée Live
Volume 1, No. 1/Winter 2011

MANAGING EDITOR
PUBLISHER

Chris Pappas

GUEST EDITOR

Rebecca Pappas

VOLUME EDITOR

Chris Pappas

POETRY EDITOR

H.R. Johnson

PUBLISHING INTERNS

Anthony Vacca
Stuart Norman
University of Montevallo

DESIGN /LAYOUT

Chris Pappas

COVER

The MFA School
An original work donated by writer and artist,

Barrett Travis

Mêlée Live

POCKET EDITION

No. 1

WINTER
2011

USPOCO BOOKS
ASHEVILLE, NC

Mêlée Live

is published three times a year, in conjunction with
Mêlée Live Monthly: a new pocket-sized magazine which
includes one poet, one story and one essay or translation in each issue.

Mêlée Live and **Mêlée Live Monthly** are published by **USPOCO BOOKS,**
the publishing division of **us poetry company.**

USPOCO BOOKS
us poetry company
15 Allesarn Rd
Asheville, NC 28804

uspoco.com
ManuFacturedArtists.com
uspocobooks@gmail.com

S U B M I S S I O N S

Mêlée Live Monthly: Submissions read year round. <u>We only guarantee a response if accepted</u>. After three weeks, if you have not heard from our staff, you may inquire via <u>one</u> email on the status of a submitted work.

Send all submissions (**five to ten pages of poetry, one story or one essay**) to **uspocobooks@gmail.com**. <u>Include month, genre and author's name in the subject line</u>. Submissions may also be considered for publication @ **ManuFacturedArtists.com**, *a blog of the arts*. **Do not include contributor notes or bios, for we do not publish them.**

Mêlée Live: Most issues are themed. In un-themed issues, submissions are solicited. *Mêlée Live* has no open reading period. If submitting a relevant work for a themed issue, send your submission, in any format, to **uspocobooks@gmail.com**. <u>We only accept email submissions</u>.

THE NEW ROTATING EDITORSHIP: Each volume of *Mêlée Live* includes three issues published over one calendar year, **January***ish*, **April***ish* and **September***ish*. Editorial duties are passed on each year (method to be determined by current editor), including full creative control of the magazine for all three issues of the volume. The magazine may be housed any where in the US, provided certain guidelines are met in documenting all agreements/contracts for a given volume.

For more information on **THE NEW ROTATING EDITORSHIP** (or to apply for the editor position for **Volume 2**), email The Editors at **uspocobooks@gmail.com**.

Mêlée Live

POCKET EDITION

Issue 1

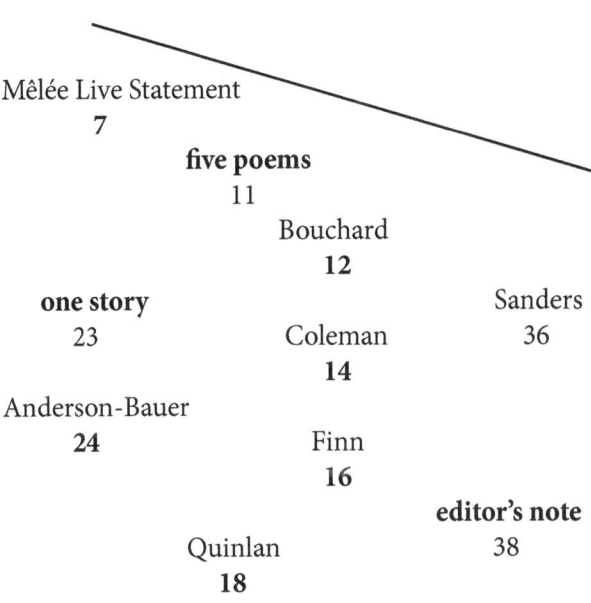

The Mêlée Live Statement

Everybody's been asking what the "live" is all about in *Mêlée Live*. The answer is two-fold. First, "live" is a decree of life—a command to live, as to a child who had quit breathing. Live *Mêlée* Live! Or "Life! Give my creation life!" This was Gene Wilder's cry in *Young Frankenstein*, when the doctor demanded the lightening come down.

Second, and most relevant to our approach this time around, the staff of *Mêlée Live* is composed of talented young thinkers and artists interested in, and dedicated to, exploring the new living connection which exists in a majority of lives today through emerging technologies. These technologies—many of them straight out of the science-fiction genre (which is often quite accurate at predicting specific details of future societies)—allow people to interact without the person(s) with whom the interaction takes place being physically present. One may even say these technologies encourage such interactions.

Telephones provide living connections. Live video may provide living connections. But we are mostly interested in the written bursts, as opposed to the verbal bursts at the heart of traditional modes of live communication.

There are at least two significant characteristics of these bursts worth mentioning here. The first is born in structure. Exchanges within the live connection are structured primarily through limitations placed on language by the particular mode of technology through which the burst occurs. For example, Facebook status updates, texts and

Tweets are limited by the number of characters the sender is allowed to employ (including space, the character of nothing). These characteristics are notable also because the focus has shifted in just a few years from considering the number of words present in a document (e.g., letters, telegrams, newspaper and magazine articles, etc.), to the number of characters in a burst. Poetic movements in the 20th century often sought to see poetry beyond or beneath the fundamental linguistic unit of the "word." Technology has succeeded where most of those movements, or schools, failed.

The term "burst" also implies a level of spontaneity present in the exchange. This is sometimes a true impression, but other times bursts are meticulously crafted to appear spontaneous. In either case, a change is occurring in the aesthetic of our daily written communications. These changes center on the need for an economy of language, which existed almost exclusively in poetry (and perhaps the telegram) in the last century. Language, through the necessity of the written modes now used to communicate, is moving toward an aesthetic which has nearly always existed in written poetry. The strict form of traditional poetic structures has forced poets toward an aesthetic of economy for centuries.

The second interesting characteristic of these bursts does not involve a shift in aesthetics directly, but a shift in the consciousness of the poet who is hooked in. Every stage of communication within the living connection is permanently documented. Every exchange, or burst, is stored in some database on some server somewhere in the interweb. So young writers and poets will have far less say in the legacy of persona they leave behind. You may have a publicist, and have your final drafts lined up in pairs on the shelf with all the reviews and letters, etc. You may consider this often and die knowing you are pleased with the impression you've constructed to leave behind. But some ambitious college student will, if you are successful enough, dig up those exchanges you wanted to bury along with the skeletons you managed to keep mostly hidden for an entire life. They won't find the real you locked away in fascicles or drawers. They will find you crouching next to a file by a character you thought you deleted. You will be there waiting to be discovered and "undisguised." They may make you truly naked and lower you down in the spotlight, on the town square of the living connection; the hidden you will become the most viewed item on the You Tube of tomorrow.

The live connection, therefore, forces a shift in self-consciousness, as well as in aesthetic.

The medium is, to some degree, actually the message. The delivery method has become at least as relevant as what is being delivered.

While the staff of *Mêlée Live* will be exploring the new living connection, it also recognizes that part of being "live" is awaiting the arrival of slow moving, visceral media, such as traditionally distributed magazines and newspapers. This is a truly live interaction (juxtaposed to the now comprehensive virtual world—which creates the need for conceiving and growing our virtual selves, who've become as essential to our personas as our so-called real selves).

Thus, *Mêlée Live* will be delivered in multiple modes. The print edition will be an expanded and updated version of the tabloid style format of the original *Mêlée* magazine. The online editions will explore the living connection in several surprising and unprecedented ways.

We have a few things planned to begin. But after that, the live connection will dictate the course and the mode of travel, for exploration cannot occur if the territory is already familiar through the maps of previous generations. We are embarking on a journey together, you and us.

Welcome back to the mêlée, and thank you for participating in the live connection. If you are reading this, you are in it, and a living connection is by nature unpredictable.

You are now the audience and the show. And it is only through you that we can conjure up the magic to make *Mêlée Live*.

The Editors
August 23, 2010

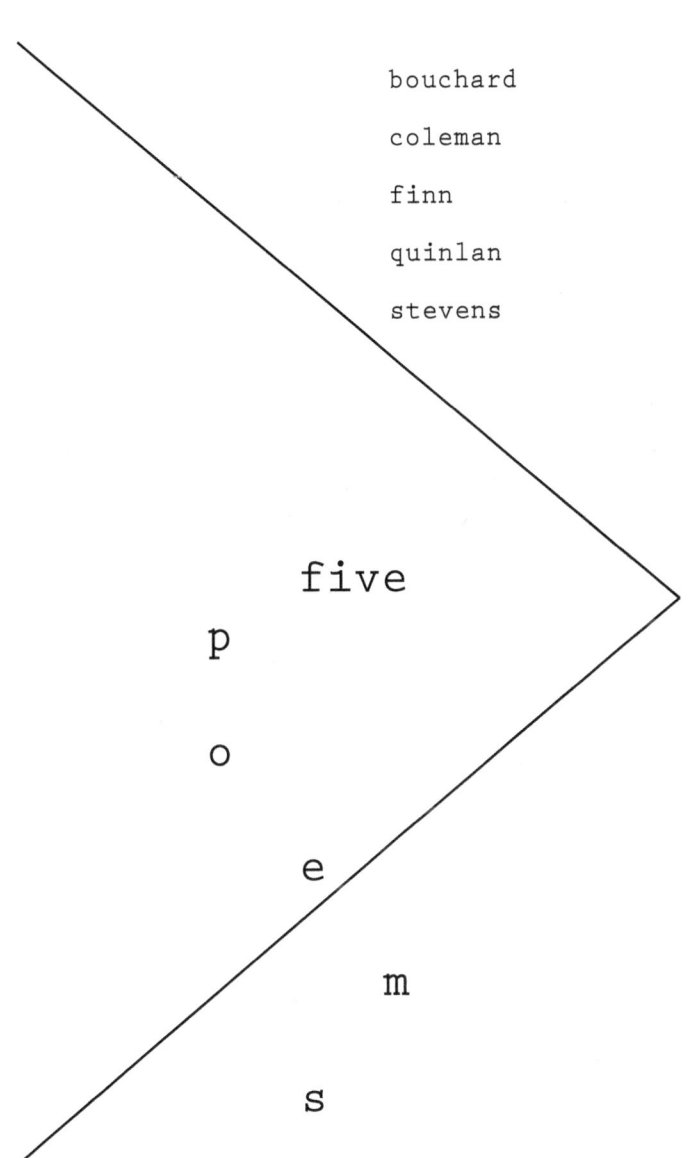

bouchard

coleman

finn

quinlan

stevens

five

p

o

e

m

s

J. R. Bouchard

ROSEMONT COLLEGE

Briefly describe the process you went through applying to MFA programs.

Bouchard: Applying was difficult, absolutely. I was in my final semester of undergrad and trying desperately to stay awake to my future and my next steps. I first made a list of what was important to me in terms of MFA programs. I wasn't tied down to anything, so I applied all over the country, sought out the best faculty and aimed high. Being a poet and neurotic meant every detail counted, and in the moment, nothing else mattered. The only problem I ran into was not believing in my writing, or at least I didn't think I was experienced enough. I applied to 12 schools, all of different calibers, and rejection after rejection, I found a few options waiting for me. I'm not sure I'd change anything now, though—even the minor heartaches that come with being a writer.

Ancestry

You study Yiddish for your ancestors—
Your tongue is your grandfather, his father,

and all the fathers and mothers you never knew.
You hold centuries in your mouth, carrying

an entire lineage on teeth, headstones
that descend back into the earth. Your gums are strong.

Their names and dates are unrecognizable, replaced
by generations reversing the language their mouths

were shaped to speak, sculpted in womb days.
Your lips grew into knowing like the separated continents

grew into forget. When you speak with your native
tongue, your voice is the wind.

Jen Coleman

HOLLINS UNIVERSITY

What poem, story, etc. made you want to be a writer?

Coleman: My mother took me to the library a lot when I was a kid; I was almost always reading. I started writing stories when I was 8 or 9 years old, but it was Yeats, whom I discovered at 13, who made me realize I wanted to write poems. I don't know why I picked up Yeats at 13—in retrospect, that's pretty bizarre. Then, when I was 15, I got the *Complete Poems of Emily Dickinson*, and that really set me off. I carried that book everywhere. I spent my time in high school reading and churning out multiple (really, really abysmal) poems per day—right up until the day I dropped out.

The Waiting

I am so wise I had my mouth sewn shut.   Berryman

These days we toe at a tenuous rift.
I sit. Your eyes, green-lit, survey the edge
and hesitate for fear that it might slip

to fated epicentre. Threads constrict
familiar famine's neophobic dread—
the days synch-full, tenuous. And this rift

goes lined by text and blood. Darkening, crypt-
ic nights all through which we forever hedge
in terror the fault should suddenly slip,

loose the years' searing swell. Which side will shift
first? What crack in the dried dirt, what ridges
rise cataclysmic, blue, along the rift

deep between us. We must be narcissists
after all that has and hasn't been said
to think our caution can prevent this slip

to present. Earth moves, dear, and continents
fit violent, gorge divides. They are not dead.
We flit the line, toe a tenuous rift
and hesitate, stitched tight, when we should slip.

Kevin Finn

CARLOW UNIVERSITY

Ask yourself the one question you hoped we would ask, which we did not ask? Then please answer your question.

Finn: *Are you nervous about the future of the arts, specifically that of poetry?*

No. The human spirit will prevail through adversity, and the poet will always be called upon to be its voice.

Protest at Tiananmen Square

I've witnessed him, erect before the machine
of war-twisted like a house on fire, the lame
tendency of smoke to rise, or carry itself
on the wind.

The act alone,
itself a lawlessness, a rabid animal
all its own, poised on

the wreckage, the pulse, waiting for it, as it
        creeps in, creeps in to a violent beat—
the kick, doubling, the tank speed doubling.

And its only recourse is a great echo,
an eagle cry; a slow diminish, an accent
on will alone-no recourse for gentle things,
where love is, where the family gathers to eat.

He blossoms like a lily, marked by the road beneath
him, to serve his will, alone.

Jess Quinlan

HOLLINS UNIVERSITY

What poem, story, etc. made you want to be a writer?

Quinlan: I attended a wonky little Southern Baptist school for most of my education. They were big into censoring what we read, so I didn't get a lot of exposure to literature that wasn't straight up *Bible* or the *Chronicles of Narnia*. (Both of which explain my developing neurosis over talking animals.) Somehow, when I was in the seventh grade, Browning's "My Last Duchess" slipped in through the cracks. We generally weren't supposed to read about stuff like murder unless it was the reasonable Baptist kind with rocks and lightning, so I still remember the crazy pleasure at "getting" the poem. It sounds funny now, but at that angry, confused, and horny age of pubescence, "My Last Duchess" epitomized subversion to me, which is still one of the qualities about poetry that I most dearly treasure.

Catalog of Signs

A season for small finger injuries: Venus
slipping or the way the dead burdock
blacken beside the road and then
are one day gone. The goldfinch return
to the boxwood, finery threaded along the ridge.
Gravestones crack in the new cold, the frost breaks
like tissue paper underfoot. It might be
how this bird disappearing into the collapsed
hay wheel is a shrike: little butcher
who strings the mice and bumblebees
on barbwire. I know if we opened the red cedar,
it would run dark with carpenter ants
which would mean something or nothing
depending on what it was we needed.

Todd B. Stevens

ROSEMONT COLLEGE

What poem, story, etc. made you want to be a writer?

Stevens: It is something that haunts me, as I remember neither the name of the poem or the poet. When I was in fifth grade, I had just transferred to a private Quaker school in Pennsylvania, Newtown Friends. At one point, a trailer was parked in our lot, under the auspices of the PA council of the arts, I believe. It had a series of poems in it, matched with photographs, a project I'd now think of as ekphrastic.

One had an enormous influence on me. I at the time was reading Vonnegut, old sci-fi books I got from my grand-father, anything else I could lay my hands on. This was a way of using language I had never thought of. It didn't really make me want to become a writer, but it was inter-esting. I spent much of my early life avoiding being bored. This was suddenly something very intriguing, important, but not easily understood.

I tried to memorize it, going back to that art trailer over and over, and when I almost got it . . . just about had it . . . . One day the trailer went away off to some other school. I doubt I'll ever find this notional poem, but I started reading poetry to re-create that feeling. "Oh, my." This is interesting.

Elegy for the World Trade Center

New York is showered in ash and fire
I can't look away, walk down the hall
to the back room, where my father is dying
burned from within, his failing body.

Look away, walk down that hall.
On the screen bodies are falling
burned from within, his failing body
my father waits with his eyes closed.

On the screen bodies are falling.
The hospice nurse said he won't wake up.
My father waits with his eyes closed.
If could I tell him, would he want to know?

The hospice nurse said he won't wake up.
But I want to go, turn on his television.
Should I tell him, would he want to know?
The fire, the smoke, the bodies falling.

I want to go in, turn on his television,
the planes fly again and again burn.
The fire, the smoke, the bodies falling,
Seven billion people watch, breathless

The planes fly again and again burn
I would tie him to something outside this room
Seven billion people watch breathless
he sightlessly falls away from himself.

Tie this to something outside the room
the back room, where my father is dying.
As he falls away from himself, sightless
New York is showered in ash and fire.

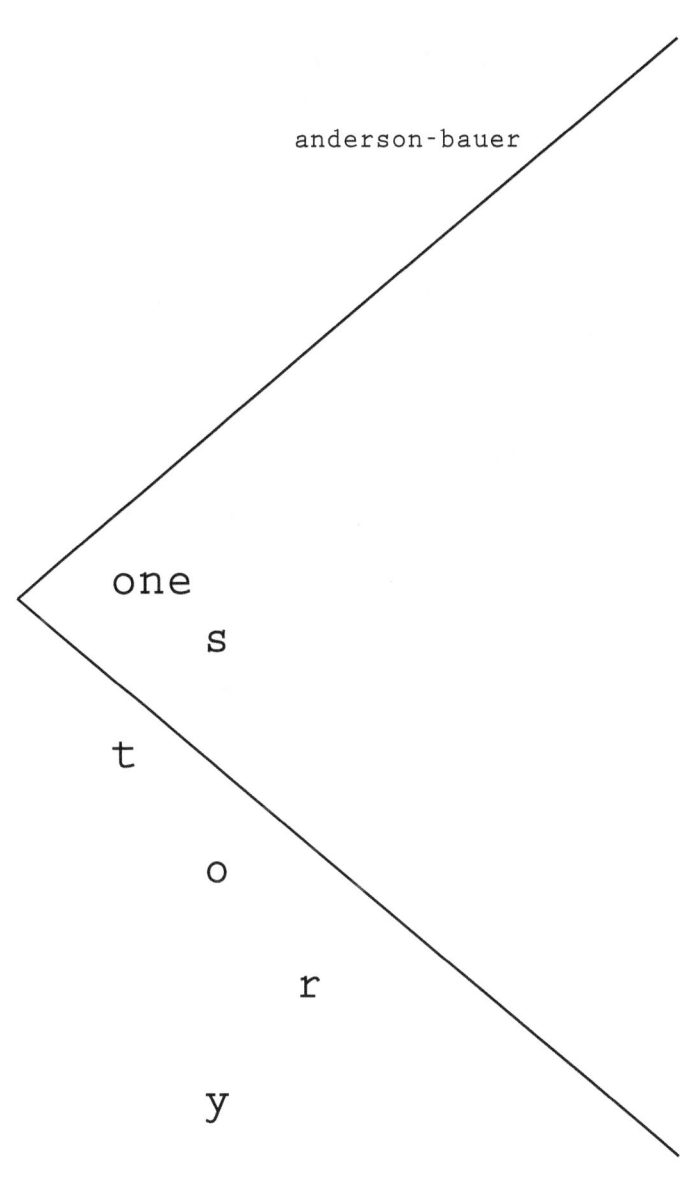

anderson-bauer

one
s

t

o

r

y

Kaj Anderson-Bauer

UNIVERSITY OF ARKANSAS

Ask yourself the one question you hoped we would ask that we did not ask? Then please answer your question.

Anderson-Bauer: *What drawbacks have you found in the MFA experience?*

I think it's true what they say about MFA programs creating a kind of rigid standard for what a short story should do and how writers should put them together. Sometimes I wonder if short stories only exist in their current form because that's what they teach in MFA programs. It gets me down, but I think it's been helpful for me. It's given me a wall to push against. I know what I don't want to write now, and that makes it easier for me to work out where I think writing ought to go—for myself at least.

Five Short Histories

I.

The prophet Muhammad could not sleep. Even during cool summer nights, like this one, his face and neck burned. He put on his robe and went across the garden to the room where his grandsons Hasan and Husayn slept. As the aged prophet walked toward their chamber through the garden, passing under the clear night sky, he looked up. Certain stars seemed out of place—as if the world's axis had silently shifted in the night. He didn't know what it meant. He found his two grandsons sleeping in their chamber. The nurse was asleep in a small bed by the doorway. The prophet moved quietly through the room to where the boys lay. He picked up Husayn, because he was still small and easiest to carry. The boy did not stir when the prophet picked him up. Muhammad wrapped the child in a blanket and carried him outside into the garden.

The great prophet sat with his back to a copse of balsam and cedar trees. The smell of the trees calmed him, and the weight of his grandson was a comfort, not a burden. He wrapped the baby tightly in the blanket and rocked the child in his arms, close to his chest, as he considered the stars. They were out of place. God's will was unclear. Suddenly, the prophet felt dizzy. The sky appeared to him as if through a deep tunnel. He saw, written in the black space between the stars, the name of an angel, and a terrible face. The angel began to speak, but her words were in a strange language. Then Muhammad saw the future—bloodshed and an indecisive God, the squandering of power, and deaths—so many people would die. Husayn began to cry in the prophet's arms, and the angel disappeared. Muhammad realized that he had been squeezing the small boy.

Forty-eight years after the death of Muhammad, the new Caliph's army surrounded Husayn and his followers in the desert. Even though the army's commander, Hurr ibin Yazid, had been instructed to destroy Husayn and his small band of supporters, he was afraid to do battle with the last heir of the great prophet. So instead, he circled their encampment and waited for thirst to kill them. After a week, Husayn came from behind the battle lines holding his infant son above his head.

"Can none of you spare a drink for my little boy?" He called out.

He intended this gesture to be like a mirror, so that the soldiers might see their cruelty—he might as well have said, "I am your brother, and this is your son," but they misunderstood the message. Some of the archers thought he was calling upon God to strike them down, and in their panic, they filled the baby with arrows. Husayn had no water to wet the sand, so he dug a shallow grave with his sword and covered the baby with his own tears. A few days later, commander Hurr ibin Yazid became impatient and massacred Husayn and his followers. They beheaded everyone and left the bodies where they fell.

Later that month, Hurr ibin Yazid called his son to his tent. Since the massacre, the commander had slipped into a dark silence.

"I have driven myself toward hell," he told his son. "I have obscured the way of God, and yet, the angels remain silent. What are we to do when the will of God forces us onto paths of evil?"

The boy listened while his father spoke, but the words meant nothing to him. When his father stopped talking, he went to his own tent and drank some water. By nightfall, he had mostly forgotten about it.

II.

Kurt von Sigel became the Third Reich's greatest marathon runner in 1937 when he won major victories in London, Rome and Berlin. A known gambler and womanizer, von Sigel's government stipend quickly ran out. As a minor celebrity, he did not think it unreasonable that his government stipend should be increased. After a few inquiries, he discovered that the Fuhrer himself was one of von Sigel's admirers, and wanted to meet with him to discuss his stipend. He received train tickets in the mail.

On the train to Berlin, Kurt von Sigel was looking out the window, admiring the lush autumn foliage. A light rain began to fall, and through the mist, it was like looking into a dream world. In his mind, von Sigel saw himself and the Fuhrer sitting at a table. The Fuhrer was smiling and laughing, and they were drinking wine and eating meat together. Then the dream changed; the leader of the Third Reich began to cough. The Fuhrer's face turned red, and he put his hands on the table, heaving, but no air came out. Von Sigel saw himself panic and call for help, but none came. Soon the Fuhrer stopped coughing and rolled to the floor. Von Sigel saw himself run from the Fuhrer's office.

When the vision passed, Kurt von Sigel felt sick. In his experience, dreams came from memories and past events; his mind never created anything new—and what he'd seen, it was new, and therefore not of his mind. It was a warning, he decided. There was no denying it—this was a warning from God. He mopped his forehead with a handkerchief and walked down the hallway of the bumping train to relieve himself.

§

Kurt von Sigel checked into his hotel room, and without fully unpacking his bag, he went for a run. He ran for miles through the streets of Berlin. None of the people recognized him, even though his face was well known at that time. Sweat poured off him in waves. God did not want him to see the Fuhrer. That at least was clear. The dream required him to be present when the Fuhrer choked and died, so if he didn't go, he could possibly save the Fuhrer's life. But he could not refuse to appear at this meeting; it would be the end of him—the end of his family. And who could say? Maybe if he refused they would arrest him and take him to the Fuhrer anyway, and he would have prevented nothing. As he ran, he began to pray for another dream or maybe someone to guide him, but nothing happened.

When he returned from his run, he went down the street and bought a bottle of expensive Swiss brandy. He took it up to his room and got drunk. It was night by then, and a stiff autumn breeze blew through his open window, though von Sigel was not cold. He called the porter and asked him to bring a bowl of strawberry ice. Standing there in the dark, he thought of his brothers, somewhere in France, and his father, back in Dresden. They would think him a coward, though he knew that he was one of the greatest patriots ever to live. Then he threw himself from his fifth story balcony.

III.

The Emperor Constantine entered Rome for the first time in 312 AD. He rode through the streets with the head of his rival, the late Maxentius, on the tip of his spear. It was October, and the rains had already begun. The people of Rome welcomed him, and there was a parade in his honor, though the rain did not subside. His helmet bore a new insignia, a sign of the new Christian god.

As he rode through the rain, he thought about the woman who his stewards had brought to his tent the night before. He couldn't remember her face, and that bothered him. It was as if she didn't have a face at all. He remembered the curve of her flanks, and the way it felt to grab her from behind, hands digging deep into the flesh of her pelvis until he gripped her very bones. He could have ripped her apart with his hands, but he could not remember her face. The crowds roared with measured enthusiasm as the rain began to pick up. He began to put different faces on the woman in his mind—the face of a sheep, the face of a bear, the face of his rival, the late Maxentius. Then the rain got so heavy that the emperor lost his train of thought entirely.

At the height of the parade, as they approached the great civic center of Rome with the statues and the buildings, and the wide paved streets, the emperor saw a black rain cloud above him. Then the cloud trembled and ripped open before his eyes. Twelve spears tore through the flesh of the black cloud, cutting it like an apple, revealing a pure white milky center. Then, from the wisps of white silk came twelve angels with the faces of snakes and twelve satyrs with the faces of babies. They came down from the cloud and formed a circle around the emperor. No one at the parade seemed to take notice. He heard the voices of God whisper in his ear. The voices told him of a deathbed and a funeral some twenty-five summers away. It spoke of a fractured empire and the mere ember of a dynasty. "Is it true power," the emperor wondered, "to be the puppet of such a god?" But the thought quickly left his mind. As soon as the parade was over, he ate a quail and forgot all about it.

§

The emperor Constantine lay on his deathbed in Nico-media—he did not have the strength to travel back to Constantinople. All of the physicians and priests agreed that he would die within the next week. One advisor mentioned certain signs in the heavens; another said that he could feel the emperor's heart slowing, but whether the cause was on heaven or earth, the emperor did not care. That afternoon, he summoned his eldest son Claudius, but his advisors told him that Claudius was in Rome. His other two sons were in Persia. Constantine prayed to God that he would live long enough to tell his son a few small secrets—plans, theories and hopes that the emperor had kept hidden from everyone, things that only a son could understand.

It was springtime, and birds were hopping around in the garden. The emperor asked two of his guards to help him walk outside to see the flowers. They took him through the trees and lilies in a wide arc before he lost consciousness. They carried him back to his room, and he died during the night.

IV.

Captain Garrett Rolf became anxious when his ship, *The Antelope*, lost its way somewhere in the gulf of Mexico. He and his crew had been trying to privateer French merchant ships sailing into Louisiana country. They'd left Halifax two months ago, but they had found no ships. Now they were short on food, and their fresh water was nearly gone. Captain Rolf hadn't told the crew he was lost, but at night he heard them grumbling in their quarters. They probably suspected.

One night, when Rolf went below deck to his room, he

heard voices through the walls—singing voices. At first, he thought that a few of the boys had robbed his liquor supply, but soon he realized that they were not the voices of his crew. These voices were familiar to Rolf—he knew from another life. He recognized the voice of his older sister, his wife and his son. There were other familiar voices, but those three brought him close to tears. They sang the song of his life. He stayed up for hours listening to them. They began by singing about his birth, his mother and their farm by the sea—then his young life, the woman who he'd met one night in Boston at the docks, the man who he'd sliced from scalp to chin, then pushed into the sea to drown. His wife, her blue dresses, and his son's little hands—the voices didn't leave anything out. When they had sung the story of everything in his past, they began to sing his future. The song quickly reached a tremendous crescendo, followed by a long mournful note. Finally, the voices gave way to silence. Captain Garret Rolf plunged into the deep wakefulness of a man who fully understands his own death. He would not sleep for three days. Finally, he would collapse from exhaustion, and two of the crew would carry him to his room.

§

There had been a dispute over direction. Captain Rolf had been trying to steer them east to Cuba, but a few of the boys thought they were much closer to New Orleans. The dispute finally came to mutiny, late on one hot afternoon. The boys had gotten together about fifteen men who now stood defiantly on deck before their captain, not saying anything, just standing there. A few of the older, more experienced sailors joined them, and that was how it happened. In the end, they all united against him, even his old friends. To Captain Rolf, everything went completely silent as he stared back at them. The sound of the sea, the creaking of the boat, the bang of the sail—all were drowned out by the steady hum of his fear. The song had told him he would be helpless. He thought of his son and decided not to fight back, because even if he killed some of them, it couldn't change the song, and these men had families, too. They tied him up, and when the storm hit later that night, two of the crew tossed him overboard.

V.

Mumtaz Mahal, "The Jewel of the Palace," married Prince Khurram when she was 19 years old. The court astrologers selected their wedding day years in advance, to be most auspicious for a happy marriage. Their love became famous throughout the kingdom. It even became a matter of gossip in the social circles of Agra. People wondered if it was decent for Prince Khurram to love his new wife so passionately and spend so much time in her company. After all, how can a king love a woman and his people?

Thirteen years after their marriage, Prince Khurram led a bloody rebellion through the southern kingdom, bringing war to both his father and brother. Three years later, when Mumtaz was 35, Prince Khurram ascended the throne to become Shah Jahan—"The King of the World." Mumtaz stayed by her husband's side during his campaigns, though the travel exhausted her.

One evening, in the town of Burhanpur, Mumtaz grew uncommonly weary. She was nearly ready to give birth to another of the Shah's children, and this baby had been particularly difficult to carry. That evening, Mumtaz retired to her chambers early. As sleep took hold of her, the air in her room began to shift. A hot wind blew through her windows. She heard voices in the wind calling her name, but Mumtaz found that she could not answer. Then a warmth began to spread from her genitals across her body, and she experienced a pleasure like none she had ever known on the perfumed couches of the Shah. At that moment, Mumtaz didn't care about any of it. I could die here, she thought, and none of it would matter, the children, her husband, the war—none of it. Then her eyes clouded over, and she saw the great prophet himself sitting under a copse of cedar and balsam, rocking a baby, weeping. Mumtaz died three weeks later, bearing the child.

When she died, Shah Jahan cursed himself. Perhaps, he thought, her death could have been prevented. After all, nothing was beyond his power. If only he had received a warning, some kind of message or a sign, he could have saved her from death. He wept freely everywhere he went and quickly fell into a deep private sorrow.

§

Twenty-six years after Mumtaz' death, Shah Jahan became ill. Sensing that their father's time was near, each of the Shah's sons took up arms, and another civil war began. Some of the Shah's children died in battle, and some beheaded their brothers. Shah Jahan watched in horror as his children tore the chambers of the world apart. After a year of war, his third son, Aurangzeb, took control of the palaces in Agra and put his father under house arrest.

Shah Jahan's prison was a palace, built of sandalwood and ivory. The building was small, but most of his servants remained with him, and he lived in reasonable comfort, though the guards did not let him leave. He grew lonely in his sweet smelling prison. He had found no companion to match Mumtaz in all the years after her death, and only his daughters could calm him when he wept for her.

§

After eight years of house arrest, Shah Jahan died. His daughter Jahanara planned a funeral for her father that included a colorful procession of all the nobles and their families through the streets of Agra, and there would be a collection of money for the needy. Prince Aurangzeb did not wish to pay for such a funeral, so the plans were canceled. Soon after his father's burial, Aurangzeb renamed himself Alamgir, which means, "Conqueror of the Universe."

Five *Short* *Histories*

S O U R C E S

Melvyn, Bragg. "Sunni and Shia Islam." *In Our Time.* BBC, 25 06 2009.

Barnes, Timothy. *Constantine and Eusebius.* Cambridge: Harvard University Press, 2006.

Preston, Diana, and Michael Preston. *A Teardrop on the Cheek of Time: The Story of the Taj Mahal.* Doubleday, 2007.

Ed Sanders

The Editors of the second issue of *Mêlée* magazine published a variety of work by Ed Sanders. We contacted him several months back about an email interview for this issue on "The MFA School." After a few scattered exchanges of questions and ideas about the school, Ed Sanders sent the following response:

The problem is that your list of questions is way far out of my personal experience.

I would never have taken a poetry workshop or writing class.

I instead studied specific poetries, through classes at NYU, a course in 1. Greek lyric poetry, 2. Chaucer, 3. The Iliad, 4. The Odyssey, 5. Herodotus, 6. Plato's Republic, and then on my own, Middle English literature, then intense personal studies in Olson, the Beats, Pound, Eliot, et al.

but never as part of a formal preparation to teach.

I deliberately turned down oodles of job offers over the years to become a teacher and a professor.

And, now that I am more or less retired, completing my final books, I have few ideas what "the poetry world" in America actually is, other than it's much more spread out across the nation than when I was a kid (when it was more or less San Francisco and New York, plus maybe New Orleans and places like Chicago). Now, there are reading series, open mikes, literary scenes in small cities all over the U.S.A.

Poets wash ashore in colleges all across the U.S., and teach/write/have long summers, and complain for 40-50 years, then retire.

Other poets make a living doing this and that. That's me. No grading of exams, no faculty intrigue, no brain-grabbing students, no pension, no university health care.

Ah Sunflower, weary of time.

EDITOR'S NOTE on *The MFA School*

To Become an American Poet

Chris Pappas, Editor

You must hate poetry. You must
work some practical
~~blue~~ white-collar/job. Want to
want to succeed. They will call you
Philistine. And be right about you. You
must do this for years or decades. You will
eventually think something is missing. From
you. Who you are. You must need to become
im-mortal in a sense greater than leaving your name
with a few lines of off-spring. Decide that you are
far too important to waste. You must realize your own
value to the world.

Then you will try everything, including poetry. But paint-
ing too, and music—many instruments—everything you
can get your hands on. You will now latch onto people
who have what you want. Most of them you despised to
start with for their certainty. They can't be that certain.
Nobody's that certain—of anything—you will say.

To put something down. On a page. Or a canvas. Or the
side of a building. And you need something to put down,
too.

Perhaps you will come to see someone who needs poetry to live. Maybe that's how it finds you. Or maybe you're just a seeker to begin with, so. You eventually find your way to where it is. Whether by philosophy or religion or sex or vanity, you will end there, if you are truly—just a seeker.

You will want to know the words. Want to understand poems. Know poetry.

Finally. You must write the poems. In secret at first.

You will slip through aisles of a small used bookstore, wondering if your new favorite poets are dead; act as if you've known them for years; find a few biographies; spend most of your free time with them.

You will find out your favorite's still alive. Plan your first trip. Traveling clear across the continent to meet him. A conference in the Rocky Mountains with poets and other holy people. They will be cheering in tents outside the college. Holding rallies for poetry and compassion.

And late that night you will find him near a tree in shadow, at last. A memorial of tin and glass and wood, twisted together and suspended from the tree's branch. He flew. Just before you got to this part of the world.

But you are on *Hajj* all the way. To the edge of united states. You will climb the stairs to poetry rooms in the North Beach neighborhood. The middle of a city where something was said to have happened decades before.

You will have your first vision of poetry.

Up there you will notice the small things. Shapes of men whip from the clothes hung off the fire escape to dry. The mural of Baudelaire in the alley below. And you will learn. He saw you too.

Eventually you will climb back down. Go back to the world. Try to tell the others what it meant to be up. Out. Over there. You will fail. But they must like the poems you wrote of the experience. Because they said they do. And they grin at you. Not because they know what you saw. But because they see it in you.

One of them, who's been writing in your hometown forever it seems, will tell you: you must send your poems to poetry magazines and poetry journals. Pile up rejection slips, he'll say. That's how you know you're a poet. He says he uses them to paper his walls.

You send some poems to a journal in your town. The editor is an acquaintance from the poetry scene. You wait for the envelope you addressed to yourself. You realize you send slips to yourself. It arrives. Before you open it, you pause for a moment. Reflect that now you're doing poetry. Your first piece of wallpaper.

The mail carrier continues on; you, still standing next to the road, open the envelope—after placing the utility bills (which were stacked on top of it) back in the mailbox. Right now, you will think, nothing matters but this. **The Slip:** The college magazine would like to publish "[your self-obsessed political rant]." Neato! The Editor. You look at the name on the slip, in case it may be a misunderstanding; check the envelope again. It is definitely your sloppy hand-writing. You start smoking cigarettes and reading the words over and over, considering your own suspicions of destiny.

You will quit your bluewhite-collar work and find a way to go to your local college for free, though it's been twelve years since you earned your "Adult Diploma" when you were seventeen.

Due to your poor public school grades, you will be a Special Status Student, the student behind the desk will tell you.
> What does that mean?
> You will begin on probation.

You will become a waiter and begin studying literature, creative writing and philosophy. You will graduate with honors in exactly four years.

Your sophomore year, you will investigate M.F.A. programs. You will hear these initials (MFA) mentioned many times during your first year, but will be too proud to ask what they stand for. You will learn.

You will travel to a beach town on the east coast hoping to visit a *Master of Fine Arts* program there. They will ignore you except when they are patronizing you.

Why are you worried about this now? You're only a

sophomore, the teacher behind the desk will say. You will decide not to apply to that school, though it started as your number one choice.

You will ask the poet teaching your first undergraduate workshop to advise you on your thesis, a collection of poems. She will tell you to ask the latest hire to advise your thesis because he won the *Yale Prize*. His letter will mean more, she will say.

You will intern for her later, working on a literary journal which exclusively publishes the writing of women. You will also intern for her husband, the editor who printed your first poem, at a publishing house which specializes in guide books. You will realize that you want to be a publisher, too. That poetry and publishing are symbiotic.

Intimidated about asking the *Yale* winner to advise your thesis, you will write an imitation of one of his poems for workshop on a day he's guest teaching. He will like it. And you will ask him.

You will question your own seriousness for the next two years because it seems he puts more into his comments than you put into writing the poems.

You will learn from him how to see as a poet sees, especially in your own work. You will work on your most promising poem with him for a year and a half. He will finally say all the pieces are in place. You will be excited to send it out. Now let's work on the line breaks, he will say. It will be your first poem accepted to a major journal.

He will teach you more. Adjectives are like ketchup and should be used accordingly. Every poem is one stanza too long, and every stanza one line too long. When you need a word, walk around and look for it in the street (or in the eyes)—not in the thesaurus. If it's just the word you were looking for, it's probably not the right word. Writers don't have to be writing every day. That is just an image that writers project out of insecurity, not knowing, but only thinking they are writers, too. A writer writes when a writer writes, your adviser will work hardest to teach you. You are a writer. Watch what you do, and that's what a writer does.

But you will also learn from watching him. You will learn the most painful lesson yet, in watching how he interacts with you and your peers:

If you persist in your art, it will develop in you an inescapable attunement to the subtlety of human interaction. It is this talent that tortures working artists—you will come to understand some years later.

You will write the first undergraduate creative thesis from the English Department at your school. For the first time you will have to analyze your own poetry—as much as it is possible to do so—for a critical introduction to your work. This will be the most fruitful process of putting the undergraduate thesis together.

As you work to finish your manuscript, you will spend hundreds of dollars and a year of time applying to a slew of top-notch M.F.A. programs. The ratio of students accepted on average at the schools to which you apply will be one applicant accepted out of every three-hundred applying. You will be accepted to two of the programs.

You will have applied to one of them (the four year program) only because there was no application fee.

The process of trying to figure out which graduate school to attend will be a tough one. You will have to move out of state to attend either school. One program requires four years to complete, the other, two years. At one school, you will teach for four years and be guaranteed full funding; at the other, you will receive a similar living stipend, but you will be a teacher's assistant until the last semester, and you will be required to pay a portion of your own tuition.

You will discuss your options for months, considering the advantages and disadvantages of each program. Eventually, you will flip a coin to decide. You will attend the four year program.

You will be told by your philosophy professor (before you decide against being a philosopher) not to pay for a graduate degree in the humanities because you'll never make any money from it. Over eight years of higher education, you will have never paid a cent of tuition.

(to be continued)[1]

1   "To Become an American Poet" was translated to Turkish and initially published in the *Inner Sri Lanka Review* as Part One in a series of five articles. This is the first printed English edition.

THE **PRINT EDITION**

OF **MÊLÉE**

LIVE IS A **TABLOID** STYLE MAGAZINE OF **PO-ETRY, POLITICS** AND **ART.** EACH ISSUE IS THEMED, WITH ORIGINAL POETRY, PROSE AND VISU-AL ART WHICH RESPONDS IN SOME WAY TO THE THEME OF THE ISSUE. MÊLÉE LIVE IS

THE OFF-SPRING OF MÊLÉE MAGAZINE (CO-CREATED AND CO-EDITED BY POETS CHRIS PAPPAS AND LISA HOLMES). MÊLÉE QUICKLY (AND BRIEFLY) GOT THE ATTENTION OF THE INSIDE/OUTSIDE POETRY COMMUNITY IN 2007 WITH RE-EM-PHASIS DE-EMPHASIS OF CREDENTIALS AND ON POETRY PERFORMANCE AND INCLUSIVE, RELE-VANT CONTENT.

[or   something   like   that   ]